THE FIRST BOOK OF *Local Government*

Local Government

REVISED EDITION

BY JAMES A. EICHNER
ILLUSTRATED BY DAN NEVINS

FRANKLIN WATTS
NEW YORK / LONDON / 1976

Library of Congress Cataloging in Publication Data

Eichner, James A
    The first book of local government.

    (A First book)
    Includes index.
    SUMMARY: An introduction to the most com-
mon forms of local government including how
they are organized and the duties and responsi-
bilities of specific departments.
    1. Local government—United States—Juve-
nile literature. [1. Local government. 2. United
States—Politics and government] I. Nevins, Dan-
iel. II. Title.
JS331.E35   1976   352.073   75–43728
ISBN 0–531–00571–2

Second edition
Copyright © 1964, 1976 by Franklin Watts, Inc.
Printed in the United States of America
5   4   3   2   1

Contents

THE FIRST BOOK OF *Local Government*

Introduction

Many books have been written about county and city government in the United States. Plenty of information on how communities are run in each state is available at the local library, courthouse, or chamber of commerce. Details like that will not be found in this book. But we will tell you about some of the main forms of organization in the more than 78,000 counties, cities, towns, boroughs, villages, school districts, and special districts in the United States.

Few American communities are governed in exactly the same way because our nation is made up of fifty fast-growing and very different states. The kind of government a place has depends on its history, population, size, and geography. The businesses and industries in an area and the laws of the state in which it is located also influence the type of government a place will have. Local governments also differ from each other because the services people need are different from place to place. For example, the problems of fire protection, street cleaning, and public welfare are much different in Cook County, Illinois, whose 1970 population included the city of Chicago and was 5,488,328, from those in Livingston County, New York, which had a population of 54,041 people. New York City spends a small fortune each year to remove snow from its streets, while many southern cities, in most years, don't spend a dime on it.

Yet for all their differences, there are some basic things about most local governments in the United States that set them apart from those in other countries. In this country "local government" means local SELF-GOVERNMENT — the way the people of a community decide for themselves, through locally elected officials, what will take place within its boundaries. In most nations, local government means the way in which the national government runs the districts into which the country is divided. The people who live in these districts have little or no direct control over what goes on in them.

Let's take, as an example of this difference, control of the police. In the United States, each city and county has its own police force, which is responsible to locally elected officials. But in most other countries the police take their orders from an officer of the central government.

Another example is the school system. In the United States, the schools are run by thousands of locally selected boards of education. Abroad, the national government usually runs the schools.

The Locality and the State

The Constitution of the United States gives some powers to the FEDERAL government and saves the rest for the states. If this system continued on down the line, the city or COUNTY (a unit of government from Britain and the biggest division of a local government within a state) would have all the powers not reserved for the state. But it doesn't work that way. The city or county is *not* a miniature state. It is just a POLITICAL SUBDIVISION *of* the state. It is created *by* the state, and usually the state legislature can destroy it if it wants to. A locality has those powers given to it by the state constitution and the state legislature, and no more. For example, if by law a state board has the power to decide what movies can be shown, a city council usually cannot pass a law covering movie censorship. A county may have the power to pass laws governing the operation of autos on its highways, but it usually cannot lay down a rule that opposes a law set by a state.

Every state has general laws that give local governments certain powers — such as the power to levy taxes on real estate, to adopt ZONING ORDINANCES (they tell how land can be used within certain districts), and so on. State legislatures also ENACT (make into law) laws called CHARTERS for individual localities that request them. One city, for example, may be allowed to set up certain departments that another city may not need. And so this city must formally request the privilege through a charter.

In some states HOME RULE charters give those who live in a community a lot of freedom to decide how they shall be governed. Then, when a change is desired, these local communities don't have to go to the state legislature to get it. Changes can be made by their city councils. In most cases, the powers and duties of local government are laid down in great detail by state law.

SUBDIVISIONS
OF THE STATE

The United States has over three thousand counties. They average about 960 square miles in size, although many in the western states are much bigger. San Bernardino County, California, contains more than 20,000 square miles. It is almost as big as the states of Massachusetts, Connecticut, and New Hampshire combined! San Bernardino is several hundred times as big as Arlington County, Virginia, or New York County (Manhattan), New York. Of course, counties also vary widely in population. The 1970 census reported that more than 7,000,000 people lived in

Los Angeles County, California, but only 73 people lived in Loving County, Texas.

Most counties are divided into townships, towns, or districts. Some of these smaller subdivisions of the county have their own governing bodies and officers. Some are also responsible for local government functions like maintaining the township roads. In other states a countywide governing body is responsible for all local functions. The district or township boundaries in these states serve mainly to define the areas from which members of this county governing body are elected.

A MUNICIPALITY, or municipal corporation, is an URBAN (belonging to the city) area with its own local government. It is compact in size, with a lot of people living in each square mile. Cities are municipalities. So are smaller incorporated (created by a charter or other legislation) urban areas which go by various names — for example, village, town, or borough. Cities are usually part of larger counties, with some overlapping of local government. But there are exceptions. In Virginia, cities are entirely separate from counties. A few major cities in other states, like Denver, Colorado; San Francisco, California; and Baltimore, Maryland, are not part of larger counties.

THE COUNTY BOARD OF SUPERVISORS

The governing bodies of American counties are known by about twenty-five different names. Among them are county commission, county legislature, county board, and BOARD OF SUPERVISORS — the name we'll use from here on.

The board of supervisors usually consists of one member elected from each of the districts or townships into which the county is divided. However, in some counties, the members are elected AT LARGE, which means that each voter in the county has a chance to vote on candidates for each seat on the board.

Some boards of supervisors are huge, with fifty or more members. These are found in counties containing large cities. There may be one supervisor elected from each WARD in the city and another from each township outside the city limits.

Most counties have small boards made up of three to six members who are part-time officials. They usually hold a regular public meeting at least once a month, with other special meetings called when county business requires it. One supervisor will be chosen by members of the board to serve as their chairperson. This individual runs the meetings and may have other special duties, such as signing papers on behalf of the board. Otherwise, the chairperson is just like any other member — elected by the voters of the district in which he or she lives, with one vote on matters coming before the board for action.

The board of supervisors is the county's legislature. Like Congress and the state legislature, it has power to make laws. These laws are usually called ORDINANCES and are legally effective only within the county. Each year the board must enact a budget ordinance providing money to carry on the county's work. It must also enact ordinances fixing the tax rate on land, personal property, licenses, and other objects of taxation.

Other ordinances may cover a wide range of subjects, such as vaccinating dogs to control rabies, regulating traffic, and providing penalties for disorderly conduct and other minor offenses.

There are fewer ordinances passed in RURAL counties, which usually have a small population, than in the more DENSELY (heavily) populated counties, which have many of the problems of big cities.

The board of supervisors may spend much of its time on matters that are ADMINISTRATIVE (managerial), not LEGISLATIVE (lawmaking). For example, it may have to supervise the buying, maintaining, operating, and selling of county property, such as the jail, the courthouse, and the dump. It may hire and supervise county employees. The SEPARATION OF POWERS between the legislative and executive branches of government, so important in federal and state government, exists much less at the county level.

OTHER COUNTY OFFICIALS

Officers who are directly elected by the people, and therefore not responsible to the local governing body, do most of the work in a local government. The prosecutor (who is usually called the district attorney, state's attorney, commonwealth's attorney, or county solicitor), the sheriff, the treasurer, the county clerk, and the tax assessor (the person who determines the monetary value of property) serve in this position. In some places, the highway superintendent, county surveyor, and other officials may also be directly elected by the people.

The prosecutor, like the judges of the courts in which he or she appears, is more of a state than a local official. This is because the administration of justice is a state function. Often, however, the prosecutor doubles as legal adviser to the board of supervisors — drawing up contracts and ordinances in proper legal form, giving legal opinions, and representing the county in lawsuits. In other places, there is a separate official, usually called the county attorney, who does this work.

The sheriff is in charge of the county jail, serves legal papers for the courts, and is usually also a law enforcement officer. Sometimes there may be a county police force, separate from the sheriff's office, that performs these functions.

The treasurer receives, accounts for, and pays out the county's money. Usually the ASSESSING of property, for the purpose of raising money through taxes, is the job of another officer, the assessor.

The county clerk may double as clerk of court and also handles much of the administrative work of the board of supervisors. This entails drawing up the budget and the agendas and minutes of the board's meetings. The clerk may also make sure that proposed ordinances are properly advertised and that licenses are properly issued.

Some counties hire full-time administrators who handle the day-to-day operations of the county government. Such officials are usually found only in the more urbanized counties. Here the demand for services requires a city-type government with water, street, utility, and police departments. The board of supervisors, in these counties, is confined mainly to setting policy.

In rural counties, one of the most important officials is the county agricultural agent. This person helps farmers keep up to date on ways of producing and selling their products. This agent is usually appointed by the board of supervisors, is paid partly by the state and federal governments, and works closely with the state agricultural college.

Another important official is the county home-demonstration agent, who teaches farmers how to process foods and better care for their children.

OTHER BOARDS

In some counties and cities, specialized citizen boards do part of the work. Members of some of these boards are appointed by the board of supervisors, judges, or other state officials. Other times they are directly elected by local voters. The board of public welfare votes on applications for public assistance. The board of health makes or recommends health and sanitation regulations.

The board of elections handles registration of voters and runs the polls on election day. There may be a planning commission, which makes studies and recommendations on the physical development of the county. There may also be a board of zoning appeals, which decides how to use certain pieces of land.

Perhaps the most important single body of citizens is the board of education or school board. In some places it is appointed by the local governing body or is dependent on it for money. But in most places the board of education is more independent of the local government and is like a local government in itself. The board's members may be directly elected by the people. And it often has power to draw up its own budget and even collect its own taxes. There may be one school board for the whole county or several school districts within a county, each with its own board. There may even be a board for each school.

City Government

The city is the oldest form of organized government. Europe's first true nation, Macedonia, came into being as late as 400 B.C. For centuries before that, important cities, or CITY-STATES (an independent state made up of a city and surrounding territory), ruled themselves. They also extended their influence over other areas near and far. Later, as central national governments became stronger, major cities received, by local charter, special privileges above those enjoyed by other localities. Some of these privileges were powers of taxation, regulation of markets, and special courts. Because they were granted by the king, or sovereign, these rights were known as SOVEREIGN RIGHTS.

The sovereign still grants special charters to municipalities in twentieth-century America. It recognizes, as did rulers in ancient times, that urban areas have special problems and need special powers to solve them. In America, of course, the sovereign is not a king or queen but the state, which acts through the state legislature.

The charter of a city, town, village, or borough, and the general state laws that apply to all municipalities, usually spell out in detail how the community shall be governed.

THE CITY COUNCIL

All cities have one thing in common: a local legislature. This body of lawmakers is usually called the city council.

[11]

The United States was founded at a time when its people were afraid of the concentration of governmental power. So the processes of separation of powers and CHECKS AND BALANCES were included in our state and federal constitutions. In this way the power to make laws was separated from the power to administer them. And to make sure the legislature was doing its job fairly, the system of checks and balances made it necessary for a BILL (a proposed new law) to pass through two houses, not just one, before it became law.

The system of checks and balances was also written into city government. Most early American city councils, like Congress, had two chambers (BICAMERAL COUNCIL). The larger one might be called the common council, the other the board of aldermen. A proposed ordinance, like a bill in Congress, had to go through a committee and to the floor in one chamber. Then this ordinance had to go through the same process, in the other chamber, before going to the executive for approval or VETO.

Times have changed. The bicameral city council is now a rarity in America. The one-chamber council of today is much smaller than either house of the typical old-time council. While a few large cities have councils of twenty-five members or more, about two thirds of the cities have councils of only five to nine members each.

There has been a change in the way members of councils are selected. These people used to be elected by wards or districts. Each section of the city would elect one or more representatives, from the people who lived there, to the local legislature. In recent years, election by wards has given way in many cities to at-large elections. People in favor of at-large elections say this system tends to produce council members with broad vision who will concern themselves with the welfare of the city as a whole. They will be less likely to be concerned *only* with their own districts. Those in favor of the ward system say it brings council members closer to the people, that it makes intelligent voting easier because the voter is more likely to know the candidates, and that it makes it harder for one social or economic group to dominate the council.

The main work of a city council, like the county board of supervisors, is to enact ordinances. Except in an emergency, an ordinance usually cannot be adopted until it has been publicized. This means that the proposed ordinance, or a summary of it, must be published in a local newspaper. After its publication, citizens wishing to do so may present their opinions of it at a scheduled public hearing. This prevents secret legislation and

makes it less likely that just any ordinance will be accepted. The city council does have certain POWERS OF APPOINTMENT of other officials. Exactly what kind of powers this council has, however, depends largely on the form of government involved.

FORMS OF
CITY GOVERNMENT

For forms of government, let fools contest.
What e'er is best administered, is best.

That is what the English poet Alexander Pope wrote many years ago, and there is a lot of truth in it. An outdated, clumsy organization can provide honest, efficient, economical government if the right people are in charge. In the same way, the most modern and scientifically organized government may produce bad results if the people in charge don't do their jobs.

In the United States there are three main types of city government: mayor-council, commission, and council-manager. The individual kinds vary according to the needs and wishes of individual cities, but each remains about the same.

Mayor-Council Form
The mayor-council government used to be the most common form of government in American cities. It is based on the idea of separation of powers. Here the mayor, like the President or

the governor, heads the executive branch. It is the mayor's duty to see that local laws are enforced, and to watch over the people who run the various governmental departments. The council, like the state legislature or Congress, makes the laws.

There are two main kinds of mayor-council government. Under the "strong mayor" form the mayor, elected by the people at large, has power to veto either all or some types of legislation passed by the council. The mayor also prepares and presents a centralized budget to the council. He or she may suggest other legislation as well. The mayor appoints and removes the heads of city departments and other major executives. The council has complete responsibility over FISCAL (monetary) affairs and the making of policy. Not much power is given to specialized boards. There is a SHORT BALLOT (an election where the voters elect the mayor, the council members, and a few important officials, but other minor posts are filled by appointment).

Under the second, "weak mayor" government, specialized boards have the power to make policy in their fields, and they have the power to supervise their day-to-day operations. For example, there may be an elected board of police commissioners that really runs the police department, or there may be a separate governing board for each major department of the city.

Commission Form

Under the commission form of city government there is no separation of powers. The local governing body, called the city commission, is made up of a small number of elected commissioners — usually three or five. Together, this commission acts as a legislative body. It adopts a budget, levies taxes, and enacts ordinances just as any local governing body does. Each commissioner is also

an executive officer who runs one or more departments of city government. One may serve as commissioner of public safety, another as commissioner of finance, and another as commissioner of public health and welfare. One of the commissioners also serves as the mayor and is the CEREMONIAL HEAD of the city government. This job entails cutting ribbons to open new buildings or highways, giving keys to the city to important visitors, and attending many luncheons. The mayor in this post has no administrative control over the departments headed by the other commissioners.

Some people praise the commission form of government because it is so simple. Responsibility is fixed and cannot be passed on to someone else (as it may be under systems based on separation of executive and legislative powers). It is said to be a businesslike form of government.

Critics of the commission form of government say any well-run business would concentrate responsibility in one executive, not scatter it among five. The commission form, some say, may make things a little *too cozy,* and so encourage a kind of VOTE TRADING fairly common under the old ward system. For example, the commissioner of public safety may agree to an unfair APPROPRIATION of money to the public works department just so that the commissioner of public works will approve his or her budget. In short, some people feel that this type of city government can give each commissioner too much freedom to run the department as a one-person show. They feel this system doesn't provide any effective check of one official against another. Early in the twentieth century the commission form of government was very popular. Later on, many cities that had tried it returned to the mayor-council type.

Council-Manager Form
The newest and most important development in local government in the twentieth century is the council-manager plan. It is now the form of government in over one third of all American cities with a population of 2,500 or more.

In theory, council-manager government provides a separation of legislative and executive power. The elected council sets policy by passing ordinances. It appoints a city manager, who serves at the "pleasure of the council." This means that he or she is appointed by the council and can be removed by it. The council tells the city manager what needs to be done, and the city manager, in turn, administers these instructions. The council elects one of its members as mayor. In this kind of government the mayor has no executive power and is just another member of the council who runs council meetings and serves as ceremonial head of the city government.

It is the city manager's job, not the mayor's, to run the city government. And the council is not supposed to interfere with the day-to-day administration of the city departments. For example, council members are not to interfere with appointment or removal of agency heads or of RANK-AND-FILE city employees.

Under the "pure" council-manager form of government, the council appoints only one official: the city manager. The manager appoints, and can fire, department heads and other high-ranking officials without the approval of the council. Lower-ranking city employees are hired and fired by the heads of the agencies in which they work.

Because council members and voters in some cities do not wish to give the manager quite that much power, variations on the "pure" form of government are common. A few important full-time officials may be named by the council, rather than by the manager, in order to keep them independent of the executive branch. These may include the city auditor, who goes over the financial accounts of the various agencies; the city assessor, who decides on the value of property for tax purposes; and the city attorney, who is legal adviser not only to the manager and department heads but also to the council and the city government as a whole.

In addition, the council may appoint part-time citizen members to policy-making boards. For example, it may appoint the city planning commission, which draws up long-range plans for the development of the city; the personnel board, which adopts and administers the civil service system for rank-and-file employees; and the health, welfare, school, and library boards.

The council-manager plan of government is often compared to the organization of a business corporation. The stockholders (voters) elect a board of directors (council), which makes major policy decisions and appoints a president (manager) to run its affairs. This comparison is fairly accurate. But remember, in business and in government there is no neat dividing line between making a policy and carrying it out. In a business corporation the president often is a member of the board of directors, and other high-ranking employees may also be directors. This puts them in a position of giving orders to themselves.

A city manager, on the other hand, has no vote in council meetings, and cannot veto ordinances the council approves. But the manager may have power to propose ordinances for consideration by the council and may regularly tell the council what policies he or she thinks the council should follow.

[21]

Departments of Local Government

Regardless of the form of organization at the top, the departments of a city government below the level of council, mayor, and manager work pretty much the same. Cities vary in the number and type of services they provide and in the organization of the departments that perform these services. But a fairly typical setup will include departments of public safety, public works, public utilities, public health, public welfare, recreation and parks, planning, finance, law, and personnel. (The school system is usually a sort of local government in itself, so its functions will not be discussed here.)

DEPARTMENT OF PUBLIC SAFETY

Many cities have separate police and fire departments. It is common, though, to put both of these uniformed services, and certain other operations, in a single department of public safety. Its boss, the director of public safety, is usually appointed by the manager or mayor. The director is the boss of the police chief, the fire chief, and other bureau chiefs.

Police Bureau

Law enforcement was probably the earliest function of local government.

Today the police bureau of a large city is often broken into

several divisions. These divisions are based on the areas they cover and the functions they serve.

The city may also be divided into two or more precincts, with one patrol division responsible for maintaining order within each precinct. For example, there may be a separate traffic division with officers specially trained in auto accident investigation. In addition to doing their share of routine patrolling, traffic officers are sent to the scenes of automobile crashes. There they help the injured, talk to drivers and witnesses, and take pictures and make measurements to help determine whose fault the accident was. If it looks as if the crash was caused by a traffic law violation, the offending driver will have to go to court.

Books, television, and radio make the detective division of a police force look different from what it really is. Actually, detectives are a group of hardworking investigators whose life consists of endless, painstaking detail work. Detectives work in civilian clothes. They do not patrol. They are called in after a crime is committed, to try to find out who did it and to gather evidence against the criminal.

The police bureau may have an identification and laboratory section with people trained in fingerprinting, photography, and other investigating skills. But the police department often sends articles to the Federal Bureau of Investigation laboratory in Washington when its own equipment can't do the job.

Many police forces have juvenile divisions whose officers specialize in offenses by and against MINORS. (The police division considers a minor someone who is under sixteen.) These officers also try to stop juvenile delinquency. Like detectives, the men and women of the juvenile division usually work in plain clothes to avoid calling attention to themselves.

Mounted squads (police officers on horses) help control crowds. Besides the horse, another well-known police animal is the attack dog. It will stop a suspicious person or attack this person on command. This dog has one master and lives at home with the officer it's assigned to.

Women are being used more and more in the police department. They have desk jobs at headquarters but also work on the street. They may work in plain clothes as detective or juvenile division officers. Or they may work in uniform as traffic directors or on regular patrol duty.

Uniformed teen-agers often work as police cadets. They do jobs like checking parking meters and are given training that will help them become full-fledged police officers if they choose to.

Fire Bureau

Fire protection has come a long way from the days when privately organized companies ran through the streets pulling hose wagons. Volunteer companies still do most of the fire fighting in most counties and small municipalities. But well-trained professionals do the job in larger cities.

The fire bureau of a large city, like the police bureau, is divided into several units, or battalions, each responsible for one area. A battalion chief commands the truck and engine companies located at fire stations within one area.

At one time only men worked as fire fighters. But recently a few women have joined the ranks.

Fire fighters usually work in twenty-four-hour shifts. During the day they keep their equipment in order and stay in training. At night they sleep in the fire station, ready at all times to spring into action on short notice. When a fire is too big to be handled by one company, a second or third alarm is sounded and more fire companies rush to help.

Other departments of the city government help out during a major fire. The department of public utilities increases pressure in the water mains. It may also cut off gas or electricity near the fire. The police direct traffic and keep crowds from the fire. Later, building inspectors will decide whether the burned building is so badly damaged that it has to be torn down.

Fire fighters do more than fight fires. Many cities have full-time fire prevention divisions. Schools, theaters, office buildings, and other places are inspected to make sure they have the right fire extinguishers, sprinkler systems, fire alarms, exits, and so on. People who violate the fire prevention code over and over may be summoned to court and fined. Fire prevention people also go to the scenes of fires to try to find out what caused them. If it looks as if a fire was set on purpose, police arson investigators along with fire prevention experts, will try to find out who did it.

Fire prevention people also run educational programs in schools and before business and civic groups to teach people how to keep their community safe from fire.

Building Inspector
Buildings are safer than they used to be because of the work of local building inspectors and the adoption of a local BUILDING CODE (an ordinance containing detailed rules for safe buildings).

A contractor (person who agrees to erect a building) must get a building permit before starting to build. Plans are filed with the building inspector's office. And the design and materials the contractor intends to use must meet the standards of the local building code. If they do, a permit is issued and work can begin. Building inspectors, usually with years of construction experience, stop by the job site to make sure the work is being done correctly. Other special inspectors check the electrical work and plumbing.

The building code usually contains requirements for *old* buildings, too. When a building or a part of it, like the porch or stairs, becomes unsafe, the owner may be required to repair it. If

the owner refuses to make a building safe, the city may "condemn" it as unfit for people to live in.

The building code also requires inspectors to check all the elevators in the city several times a year.

Traffic Engineer

Each year automobile traffic becomes a bigger problem in American cities. Police can't solve this problem by themselves. So trained specialists study traffic patterns and find ways to move motor vehicles faster and more safely. Employees of the city's traffic engineering bureau run counts of the number of cars and trucks moving at various times on various streets. Electric traffic counters do much of this work. But sometimes traffic engineers also talk to drivers to find out where they are coming from and where they are going. Using this information, the traffic engineering bureau decides what the speed limits should be. It finds out

what streets should be one-way and where traffic lights and signs should be put up. It even tries to find out how long red and green lights should be on in each direction at different times of day. Traffic engineers also help set up and direct city bus lines.

DEPARTMENT OF PUBLIC WORKS

The public works department usually has more employees than any other city department. Its street maintenance division is the best known. The workers and trucks are always on the streets filling up a hole here, patching a sidewalk there, resurfacing sev-

eral blocks somewhere else. When winter comes, it is this department's job to keep the streets free of ice and snow.

Most cities do not have special work forces big enough to handle major construction projects. It is usually cheaper to hire other companies (usually private contractors) who do major street repairs, build sewage systems, and construct city buildings. These contractors are usually given the work on the basis of competitive bids. That is, each contractor carefully figures out what it will cost to do the job. Then the contractor submits this amount in a sealed envelope to the city. All the bids are usually opened publicly at the same time and are then studied by city officials. Finally, the contract is given to the lowest bidder or the contractor with the best offer.

Before large projects are undertaken, city design engineers make careful studies of the location of the proposed construction. They check to see what materials should be used in it and what kind of design it will have. When construction begins, city inspectors check to make sure the contractor is doing the job according to plan. Inspectors order that improper work be done over. City engineers approve payment of the job as it progresses. Not until the work is finished and carefully checked is final payment made.

The sewer maintenance division of the department of public

works has the important job of seeing that domestic and industrial wastes and rainwater are properly disposed of.

Cleaning the streets and disposing of trash and garbage is the work of the division of street sanitation.

The department of public works may have other specialized jobs like running a city airport, a harbor, or sometimes even operating the city's water, gas, or electric systems.

DEPARTMENT OF PUBLIC UTILITIES

American cities are in business in a big way. Most sell water and many sell gas. Some run electric plants to provide power for street lights and sometimes for sale. In recent years more and more cities have taken over bus lines and other means of transportation.

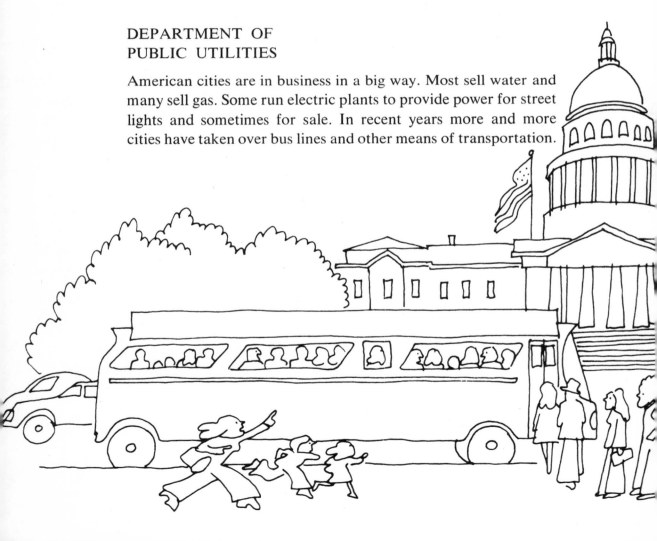

The department of public utilities is organized, on the surface, like the other departments of city government. But because this department is expected to pay its own way, its bookkeeping system may be set up like that of a privately owned utility. This department may turn over to the city treasury a sum of money equal to what its plant would produce in taxes if privately owned.

The department of public utilities will operate a plant to make water pure and will also add chemicals to it to prevent tooth decay.

Water is piped to customers through large water mains buried under the streets. Service lines connect these mains to customers' houses. The water mains and other equipment are usually designed to meet unexpected demands. For example, if there is a fire, large amounts of water will be needed in a short time.

Cities that sell gas usually buy it from a private pipeline company. But very often cities have plants of their own for manufacturing gas when necessary.

Meter readers regularly check to see how much gas, water, or electricity has been used. Then the billing section of the department will collect whatever is owed them from customers.

DEPARTMENT OF PUBLIC HEALTH

The rise of the modern city is due largely to advances in public health. The big city used to be a place where disease was widespread and plagues attacked the people who lived in it. Open sewers, heaps of refuse in the street, polluted water supplies, unsanitary markets and dwellings — all helped the spread of disease. It was not until the nineteenth century that sanitation advanced in the great old cities of Europe to the point where birth rates were higher than death rates.

Following basic rules of sanitation and building proper water, sewage, and food-handling facilities have made the city a healthier place to live.

The city health department includes at least one doctor and several nurses. Most public health work, however, is done by sanitarians. Sanitarians are inspectors who move through the city to make sure people who run restaurants, food-processing plants, nursing homes, and other places obey the rules laid down in state and local sanitation laws.

Sometimes a place is inspected in answer to a citizen's complaint. But most inspections are made as a matter of routine. For example, a sanitarian will visit every eating place in the area he or she is responsible for. Then the sanitarian will run down a detailed checklist to make sure that the kitchen is clean and that the walls or ceilings don't have cracks that may invite dirt or insects. He or she checks to see that the food is properly refrigerated, that the toilet facilities are maintained, and that the doors and windows are screened. If any of these rules have been violated, the sanitarian will order that the violation be corrected. Later on, the sanitarian will come back to make another check. If the owner ignores one or two warnings, his or her permit will be taken away, a summons to court will be issued, or both penalties will result.

Dogs can be a health problem. Sanitarians travel through the city to make sure dogs have licenses and current rabies vac-

cination tags. Those that don't may be taken to the dog pound in health department trucks.

Other divisions of the health department run clinics to give medical and dental care to people who can't pay for it. Free chest X rays are provided for early detection of tuberculosis. Clinics are held for mothers-to-be and also for babies. Some needy persons who cannot get to clinics are visited at home by city nurses. Many large cities operate nursing homes and full-scale hospitals to give free care to the poor.

Some health departments have education divisions. The people in these divisions hand out literature, hold classes, and answer questions about public health.

The city health laboratory tests and analyzes thousands of samples of blood, milk, water, and other substances that are sent in by doctors, clinics, and hospitals.

Nutrition experts give people who need it advice on their diets. The local health department also sees that sprays to get rid of mosquitoes and others insects are used, and it prepares figures on births, deaths, and diseases.

DEPARTMENT OF
PUBLIC WELFARE

At one time, running the "poorhouse" for those who couldn't make a living was the only form of public assistance. Today the city home, or nursing home, still plays an important part in the work of a modern welfare department. But the trend is to keep people in their own homes with the help of monthly assistance payments and the advice of trained social workers.

The local government votes to spend a certain amount of money each year on each of the main public welfare programs. These are aid to dependent children, the disabled, the aged, and the blind. Adoption planning, medical care, foster home care, and general relief are also among the public welfare programs. Most of the money for these programs comes from state and federal tax funds. And federal and state governments set up rules that a city or county must abide by before receiving any money.

Critics of the welfare system protest that there are people on the welfare rolls who have no right to be there. In a large city, it is almost impossible not to give public assistance to some people who are able to support themselves. But careful checking by welfare department workers will keep the numbers of these people to a minimum.

Public welfare workers are trying to help people help themselves. The idea is to give a relief check to a person *only* until he or she can be self-supporting again. Of course, some people, such as the aged or disabled, can never be self-supporting.

Welfare workers also give help to juvenile and domestic relations courts. They help furnish information about the people who are on trial. For instance, in a juvenile court case, a welfare worker might be able to supply information on a child's family situation at the time of his or her arrest. This may help explain why a juvenile offender committed a public offense and may aid in determining the discipline recommended for the particular case.

DEPARTMENT OF
RECREATION AND PARKS

For a long time, planners of cities have provided parks and other open spaces for the enjoyment of the public. Now modern cities also provide a wide variety of activities to give young people and adults something to do with their spare time. Having little to do with one's spare time has become a social problem. Work weeks are shorter, and the chances for young people to find work have become more difficult. That is why cities have plunged into the business of running swimming pools, tennis courts, baseball diamonds, and other sports facilities. Dances, chess and checkers tournaments, bridge lessons, and Halloween parties are other common city-run recreation activities.

Recreation departments are even busier during the summer months when schools are closed and many adults are on vacation. At these times temporary recreation workers, including teachers and teen-agers, help the year-round staff.

DEPARTMENT
OF FINANCE

It is the job of the department of finance to take care of money matters for a local government.

The director of finance supervises the collection of taxes and sees that a city's bills are paid. These include wages earned by city employees, payments due to contractors, and interest earned on MUNICIPAL BONDS. Finance officers must see to it that other departments do not overspend their budgets and run out of funds before the end of the year. In many cities there is also a city auditor who is responsible only to the city council. The city auditor makes sure the different governmental agencies are spending the taxpayers' money the way they should.

Property taxes are the most important single source of income for local governments. The governing body, by passing an ordinance, sets the tax rate — for example, $2 for each $100 of assessed value. The assessor may either be responsible to the finance director or be the head of a separate department responsible only to the city council. It is this person's job to decide how much money a piece of land is worth. If the property is assessed too low, the owner will not pay a fair share of the cost of local government. If the assessment is too high, the owner will pay

more than a fair share. State laws usually require property to be assessed at its "fair market value" — that is, what a willing buyer would pay to a willing seller.

In practice, most tax assessments are far below actual value. (The actual market value can change from year to year.) But this does not produce inequality if it works the same way for everyone. For example, if a house is actually worth $10,000, it makes no difference to the owner if it is assessed at full value, with a tax rate of $2 per $100, or at half its value, with a rate of $4. In either case, the owner pays $200 in taxes.

Business license taxes, taxes on theater admissions, and sales

taxes are all sources of income for local government. Income from city utilities and SPECIAL ASSESSMENTS for sidewalks, sewers, and alleys also provide income to the government. A special assessment is a charge that pays for all or part of the cost of a local improvement. This charge is placed on the property that benefits from the improvement. It is different from an ordinary tax because it can be levied only on land.

Borrowing money by issuing bonds is the job of the finance department and is an important part of local government finance. In 1972, the total debt of all American local government units, including special districts, was $120.7 *billion*. This department estimates how much money must be raised by a bond sale and then advertises it to the public. The finance department receives bids from those who want to buy the bonds and handles their actual sale. Then, as the years go by, it sets aside money to pay interest on the bonds and gives cash for them when they become due.

Major capital improvement projects, like building streets, sewers, schools, and bridges, are paid for by bond sales. The cost of these improvements is spread over many years so those who benefit from these projects help pay for them.

DEPARTMENT OF LAW

The city attorney, or city solicitor or corporation counsel, heads the legal department. In smaller communities the city attorney

is usually a lawyer in private practice who serves the local government on a part-time basis. In larger cities the city attorney devotes full time to giving advice to council members, department heads, and other officials. He or she helps draw up ordinances, contracts, deeds, and other legal papers. The city attorney defends the city in lawsuits brought against it, files suits against others on behalf of the city, and sees that ordinances are enforced. The city attorney is usually appointed by the council. One or more assistant city attorneys may be hired to share the work.

DEPARTMENT
OF PERSONNEL

The SPOILS SYSTEM used to be the rule in local government. Jobs at all levels were handed out as political favors. When an election brought a new group to power, it was common for the people in the old administration to be fired and the friends of those in the new administration to take their place. The theory was that "to the victor belongs the spoils." The evils of this system are apparent. Lazy, incompetent people kept their jobs because they knew the right people, while able, hardworking employees could lose their jobs at any time. Under such a setup, the pay received by a municipal employee might have very little to do with the job that person did.

A reform movement to set up civil service or MERIT SYSTEMS for municipal employees started in the latter part of the nineteenth century. Today, many cities and counties use merit systems at all levels below top management. Such a system provides for hiring and promotion according to a person's experience and performance. It prevents permanent employees from being fired unjustly. And it tries to equalize pay among those people doing the same kind of work.

A personnel board or civil service commission runs the merit system. Usually this board consists of citizens appointed by the council, often with one member chosen from the ranks of the municipal employees. The personnel board adopts rules that state in detail how new employees will be selected. It spells out how long they must serve to prove themselves capable of handling a job before they are hired on a permanent basis; how people are chosen for promotion to better jobs; how much time employees can have for vacation, holidays, and sick leave; when an employee can be disciplined by suspension, demotion, or dismissal; and what rights of appeal a discharged employee has. The personnel board usually hears these appeals. After a hearing, the board decides whether or not what the supervisor did was justified.

The personnel director and assistants act as a staff for the personnel board. Together they handle the day-to-day administration of personnel matters. These consist of recruiting needed workers and drawing up and conducting tests for job applicants and employees seeking promotion. The board studies all jobs in the city service to try to provide equal pay for equal work, and it runs programs that teach anything from speed reading and first aid to civil defense.

DEPARTMENT
OF PURCHASING

If the department of public works needs fifty shovels and the department of public utilities needs another fifty, it makes little sense for each department to go shopping on its own. Things cost less when they are bought in large numbers. So a centralized purchasing agency makes it possible for a city to enjoy savings like this. It also puts buying into the hands of specialists who may know more about prices and quality than a department head who has little time to spend on such matters.

The purchasing department usually awards contracts for goods and services on a competitive basis. Interested firms are asked to submit sealed bids at a set time. The bids are opened and read publicly. Then the contract is usually given to the lowest responsible bidder.

The purchasing agent's office may be combined with other centralized services to form a department of general services. For example, it might maintain city-owned buildings and motor vehicles, or it may be combined with the agencies that buy insurance and bonds, or purchase and sell city real estate.

The Public Library

The library is one of the city's most important educational and cultural institutions. A modern public library does much more than just loaning out books. Many also have good collections of phonograph records that can be borrowed. Back issues of newspapers and other material are stored on microfilm. A wide variety of magazines and research books are available. Sometimes valuable unpublished works can be found in public libraries. Many cities have branch library buildings. Some cities have book-mobiles — specially equipped trucks that stop for a few hours each week at different places throughout the city. In rural areas, bookmobiles bring books to people who have a hard time getting them.

Authorities and Special Districts

In many areas, some of the services needed by citizens are not provided by local government but, rather, by separate corporations created for special purposes. Many cities have redevelopment and housing authorities that have power to acquire land and buildings in slum areas. They do this so that they can clear the land and build low-rent housing units on it. Turnpike, tunnel, bridge, and transit authorities take care of transportation prob-

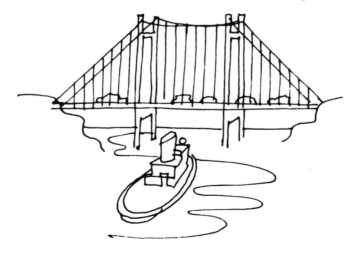

lems in some communities. Other SPECIAL DISTRICTS (as these separate corporations are called) supply fire protection, mosquito control, flood control, parks, libraries, and sewerage service within limited areas. These special-purpose organizations usually have their own governing bodies, which are appointed by the local city council or county board of supervisors. Some authorities have power to levy taxes on property within their areas. Others get the money they need by charging for the services they provide.

Planning

Problems such as traffic tie-ups, transportation failures, and poor housing are caused by lack of proper planning. Streets that are too narrow, industries that are in the wrong place and the lack of enough open space are some of the results of the failure to look far enough ahead. Past mistakes like these can't be corrected easily because the cost of tearing down and rebuilding the major parts of a city would be too high. But better planning now will prevent mistakes from being made later on. This is the work of the local planning commission. This commission is made up of a group of citizens appointed by the city council or some other local governing body and its staff of professional planners. Their job covers both long and short-range planning.

The basic long-range job is set out in a MASTER PLAN for the physical development of the community. This plan, which fills a big book, includes maps that tell where streets should be laid out or widened and where schools, parks, and other public facilities should be located. The areas that should be used for single-family homes, for apartments, for businesses, for light and heavy industry, and for railroad yards are also mapped out in the master plan.

The local planning commission, often with outside help, takes a careful look at the community. Then the buildings in it are drawn on a large-scale map. Every neighborhood is checked to see how land in it is being used. Census figures and other information are studied to try to predict the size and direction of future population growth. Now planners can map out a better design for the city because they know what its future needs are likely to be.

The zoning ordinance helps carry out the master plan. A city or county is divided into zones or districts, with the boundary of each district shown on a zoning map. This ordinance tells how land can be used in each district and classifies each piece of land in it. One classification is single-family residential. This means

that only one-family homes and structures like churches, parks, and perhaps schools are allowed here. In other zoning areas only two-family and multiple-family houses are allowed; and in other districts only places of business and industry are allowed to be built.

A structure cannot be built or changed very much without a building permit. So the zoning map is the first thing to be checked before anyone applies for a permit. The map will show quickly whether the structure the applicant wants to build is permitted by this particular ordinance.

Some zoning ordinances might class as "residential" (where homes are built) a district that already has some business or industrial offices in it. But these office buildings do not have to be torn down. Zoning ordinances therefore allow for "nonconforming uses." This means that an office building may stand in a district made up of homes. But if the office building is destroyed, the new building put up in its place must conform with (agree or meet up to) the old ordinance. In this case the new building must be a home.

Conditions change, of course. No master plan or zoning ordinance is good for all time. Every few years, there may be a major revision, or minor changes may be made in this plan more often.

For example, a person who owns property in a residential zone that borders on a business district may feel that the land can't profitably be used for a home. The owner may want to build a store on it instead. To do so, the land must be rezoned. So the zoning ordinance must be changed to include this piece of land in the business district. Like any other change in an ordinance, this requires a public hearing before the local governing body.

Municipal Growth

Each year, a greater proportion of the population of the United States becomes concentrated in its cities. As more homes, apartment houses, factories, stores, and office buildings are built, a city often runs out of living space. So the city must expand its boundaries. This is usually done by annexation (addition) of land lying outside the city limits. This process is often handled by a special type of court proceeding called an ANNEXATION SUIT. Another way of expanding is to combine two or more local political subdivisions by vote of the people who live in them.

Jobs in Local Government

There are plenty of chances for jobs in local government, ranging from unskilled labor to the highly trained professions. A modern city government needs doctors, lawyers, engineers, real estate appraisers, accountants, nurses, and employees of many other trades and professions. There are, in addition, special careers usually available *only* in government service — like those of fire fighters and police officers.

Local government service often offers less pay than similar jobs in private business. To some extent this is made up by generous FRINGE BENEFITS. (Fringe benefits include holiday and va-

cation time and retirement benefits.) In addition, a person in government service often finds that he or she is allowed more responsibility than in a job in private industry. Many Americans find satisfying lifetime careers as employees of cities, counties, and other local governments. Others find a few years of local government service gives them a good start in private business or professional practice.

There are also thousands of other jobs in local government that provide little, if any, financial reward. These are volunteer and part-time jobs as members of local governing bodies and on the many citizen boards that make important decisions in the fields of welfare, health, zoning and planning, personnel, education, and others. In recent years, women have taken over more of these jobs. Many have served as mayors or as chairpersons of county boards. Some communities have had councils consisting entirely of women.

The citizens who give freely of their time and energy to serve their communities may not be paid for their work, but they are given the satisfaction of having helped make the city or county a better place to live in. These candidates are willing to serve, in many instances, because they have the loyal backing of their friends both before and after election day.

Glossary

ADMINISTRATION. Having to do with day-to-day management, as opposed to lawmaking and other policy-making procedures.

ANNEXATION SUIT. A special court proceeding by which a city acquires additional land.

APPROPRIATION. The amount of money voted on to run a city or other organization for a period of usually one year.

ASSESS. To value a piece of land or other object in order to tax it.

AT LARGE. A method of choosing members of a legislature from the whole city or county rather than according to districts.

BICAMERAL COUNCIL. A local governing body with two houses.

BILL. A proposed new law.

BOARD OF SUPERVISORS. The governing body of a county.

BUILDING CODE. An ordinance stating in detail how houses and other buildings must be constructed. This code particularly emphasizes the safety requirements for buildings.

CEREMONIAL HEAD. An official, such as the mayor or chairperson of a county board of supervisors, whose job is or includes representing the city or county on public occasions.

CHARTER. A grant of power in which a state lawmaking body gives certain powers to the government of a city.

CHECKS AND BALANCES. A system of regulating the power of one organization by the power of another. For example, a bill cannot become a law without being approved by the two houses of a legislature.

CITY-STATE. An independent state made up of a city and its surrounding territory.

COUNTY. The largest division into which most American states are divided. In Louisiana this division is called the parish.

DENSELY POPULATED. Having a large number of people per square mile.

ENACT. To make into a law.

FEDERAL. A system of government in which some powers are given to a national or central government and others are kept by the states, provinces, and other units into which the nation is divided.

FISCAL. Relating to a budget: that is, a plan for collecting and spending money.

FRINGE BENEFITS. Sick leave, free insurance, vacation and retirement benefits, etc., that are given to a worker in addition to his or her regular pay.

HOME RULE. A system of local government in which the locality, rather than the state legislature, is allowed to decide what powers the locality may have.

LEGISLATIVE. Pertaining to the legislature of a nation, state, or locality. The work of passing laws as opposed to executive or administrative work — executing them.

MASTER PLAN. A long-range plan for the physical development of a community.

MERIT SYSTEM. A civil service system in which employees are chosen and promoted on the basis of their worth — not their political connections.

MINOR. One who is too young to be an adult. The police department considers a minor anyone who is under sixteen.

MUNICIPALITY (OR MUNICIPAL CORPORATION). A city, town, village, or other subdivision of the state. This area is densely populated, with a government of its own.

MUNICIPAL BOND. An interest bearing certificate that a local government issues.

ORDINANCE. A law passed by the legislature of a local government that has effect only in the area served by that government.

POLITICAL SUBDIVISION. A part of the state that has some powers of self-government. Some examples are a county, city, or town.

POWER OF APPOINTMENT. The right given to an official or a group of officials to choose certain persons to fill certain jobs.

RANK AND FILE. Ordinary members of a civil service system or other group of employees (as opposed to their leaders).

RURAL. Pertaining to the country, as opposed to the city.

SELF-GOVERNMENT. The system by which the people of a locality are governed by officials that they elect, rather than by officials chosen by the central government.

SEPARATION OF POWERS. The granting of some power to the legislature, such as a city council; some power to the executive, such as the mayor; and some power to the judiciary, such as the local courts.

SHORT BALLOT. A form of election in which very few officials are directly chosen by the voters. This is the opposite of the long ballot, where a large number of officials are directly elected.

SOVEREIGN RIGHTS. Special rights (such as the power of taxation) that are granted by a sovereign (a king or queen) or by the state represented by its legislature.

SPECIAL ASSESSMENT. A charge that pays for all or part of the cost of a local improvement. This charge is placed on the property that benefits from the improvement. Special assessments differ from ordinary taxes because they are levied only on land.

SPECIAL DISTRICT. A separate corporation created to provide a given area with a service (flood control, for example). The people in this area usually pay for this service regardless of whether or not the area they live in comes under the jurisdiction of another local government.

SPOILS SYSTEM. At one time when an election brought a new group to power, it was common for the new administration to bring in its friends and fire the people working in the old administration.

URBAN. Belonging to the city or town.

VETO. To disapprove.

VOTE TRADING. The practice of one member of a legislature casting a vote in favor of a certain measure in return for another member's agreement to vote for another measure.

WARD. One of the districts into which many cities are divided for the purpose of the city council.

ZONING ORDINANCE. This ordinance tells how land can be used within certain districts.

Index

City-states, 11
Civil service, 20, 46
Clerk of court, 9
Clinics. *See* Public Health and Welfare board and departments
Commission government, 16, 17–19
Commissioners, 17–19
Common council, 13
Commonwealth attorney. *See* Prosecutor
Congress, 7, 13, 17
Constitution, U.S., 2, 13
Constitutions, state, 3, 13
Construction, 28, 32
Contractors, 28, 32
Council manager government, 16, 19–21
Councils, city, 3, 11–16, 19, 20
Counties
    Arlington, 4
    Cook, 1
    Livingston, 1
    Los Angeles, 5
    Loving, 5
    San Bernardino, 3
County
    attorneys, 8
    board. *See* Board of supervisors
    Board of supervisors, 5–7, 8, 9, 14
    clerk, 8, 9
    commission. *See* Board of supervisors
    government, 1, 2, 3–10

home-demonstration agent, 9
officials, 5–9
solicitor. *See* Prosecutor
surveyors, 8

Departments of local government, 22–52
Design engineers, 32
Detectives, 24
District attorney. *See* Prosecutor
Districts, 1, 2, 5, 6, 13, 14
    special, 1, 49–50
Divisions, police, 22–25

Education, board of, and department, 10, 38
Election boards, 10
Engineers. *See* Public Works department

Farm problems, 9
F.B.I., 24
Federal government, 2, 7, 9
Finance, fiscal affairs, 17, 18, 40–43
Fire battalions, 25–28
Fire bureau and protection, 1
    See also Public Safety department
Fire prevention, 28
Fringe benefits, 53–54

General Services department. *See* Purchasing department
Governing bodies, 5

37555

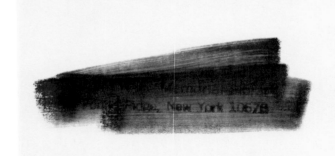

79